EYEWITNESS READERS

PROFICIENT READERS 4

GOING FOR GOLD!

Written by Andrew Donkin

London • New York • Sydney • Delhi

Let the games begin!

Once every four years, the best athletes from all over the world gather together in one city to take part in the biggest sporting event on earth – the summer Olympic Games.

Winning a gold medal is the ultimate aim of every competitor in each of the many events. Athletes spend long and often lonely years training hard for the great games.

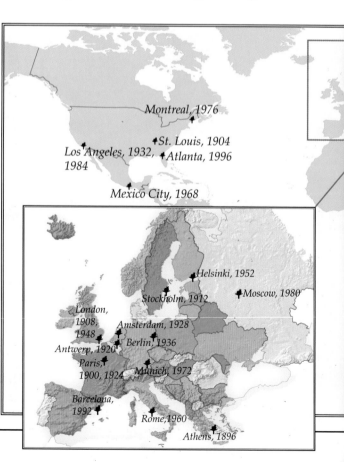

Montreal, 1976

St. Louis, 1904
Los Angeles, 1932, 1984   Atlanta, 1996

Mexico City, 1968

Helsinki, 1952

Moscow, 1980

Stockholm, 1912

London, 1908, 1948   Amsterdam, 1928

Antwerp, 1920   Berlin, 1936

Paris, 1900, 1924   Munich, 1972

Barcelona, 1992

Rome, 1960

Athens, 1896

A Note to Parents and Teachers

Eyewitness Readers is a compelling new reading programme for children. *Eyewitness* has become the most trusted name in illustrated books and this new series combines the highly visual *Eyewitness* approach with engaging, easy-to-read stories. Each *Eyewitness Reader* is guaranteed to capture a child's interest while developing his or her reading skills, general knowledge and love of reading.

The books are written by leading children's authors and are designed in conjunction with literacy experts, including Cliff Moon M.Ed., Honorary Fellow of the University of Reading. Cliff Moon spent many years as a teacher and teacher educator specializing in reading. He has written more than 140 books for children and teachers and he reviews regularly for teachers' journals.

The four levels of *Eyewitness Readers* are aimed at different reading abilities, enabling you to choose the books that are exactly right for each child.

Level One – Beginning to read
Level Two – Beginning to read alone
Level Three – Reading alone
Level Four – Proficient readers

The "normal" age at which a child begins to read can be anywhere from three to eight years old, so these levels are only general guidelines.

No matter which level you select, you can be sure that you're helping children learn to read, then read to learn!

www.dk.com

Created by Leapfrog Press Ltd

Project Editor Elizabeth Bacon
Art Editor Rebecca Johns

For Dorling Kindersley
Senior Editor Mary Atkinson
Senior Art Editor Peter Bailey
Production Melanie Dowland
Picture Researcher Jo Walton
Jacket design Chris Drew

Reading Consultant
Cliff Moon, M.Ed.

Published in Great Britain by
Dorling Kindersley Limited
9 Henrietta Street
London WC2E 8PS

2 4 6 8 10 9 7 5 3 1

Eyewitness Readers™ is a trademark of
Dorling Kindersley Limited, London.

Text copyright © 1999 Andrew Donkin
Illustration and compilation copyright © 1999
Dorling Kindersley Limited, London

A CIP catalogue record for this book is
available from the British Library.

ISBN 0-7513-6213-1

Colour reproduction by Colourscan, Singapore
Printed and bound in Belgium by Proost

The publisher would like to thank the following
for their kind permission to reproduce their photographs:
Key: t=top, a=above, b=below, l=left, r=right, c=centre

Action Plus: 14b; AKG London Ltd: 6b;
Allsport: 2, 4bl, 6t, 7t, 10t, 13, 20t, 37, 43b, 44t, 44–5b;
Associated Sports Photography: 21b, 25; Corbis UK Ltd: 8b;
DK Picture Library/National Maritime Museum: 12b;
/Robert Opie: 21t; Empics: 36b; Hulton Getty: 10b, 23;
Impact Photos/Jorn Stjerneklar: 22b;
Popperfoto: 5br, 14t, 15b, 36t, 39, 40, 42, 45t; Rex Features: 15t;
Science Photo Library: 4b; Sporting Pictures: 4tl;
Supersport/Eileen Langsley: 38t, 40t;
Topham Picturepoint: 7b, 9, 11, 24t, 43t

Additional photography by Philip Dowell, John Garrett,
Dave King, David Spence

Contents

After all that work, the athletes spend only a few hours at the Olympic Games competing against the "best of the best".

Some of the greatest Olympians of all time are featured in this book. Each one had to overcome incredible obstacles on his or her way to a gold medal.

But first, how did the Olympic Games begin?

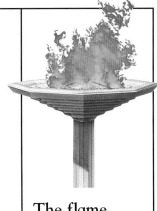

The flame
The Olympic motto is "Swifter, higher, stronger". The torch flame symbolizes this motto.

Seoul, 1988   *Tokyo, 1964*

Sydney, 2000
Melbourne, 1956

Kerri Strug
Gymnast Kerri faced an agonizing challenge at the 1996 Games in Atlanta.

5

The ancient games

The first recorded Olympic Games took place in the small Greek city of Olympia nearly 3,000 years ago, in 776 BC.

These games consisted of just a single sprint race. As word of the games spread, more people wanted to take part. The organizers soon added other events, such as long-distance races, throwing, wrestling and chariot racing.

Back track
The earliest Olympians raced on a track which was 192 metres (629 ft) long.

This illustration from a Greek vase, made in 400 BC, shows two Olympic wrestlers.

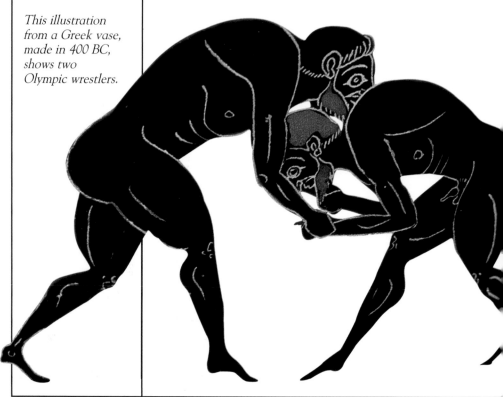

The Greek king ordered that a magnificent stone stadium be built so that a crowd of thousands could watch the sporting drama unfold.

Women were forbidden to attend the games. If a woman spectator was discovered, she was hurled off a nearby cliff.

The ancient games were held every four years until a Roman emperor banned them in AD 393. The stadium gradually fell into ruin.

Centuries later, in 1829, the ruins were discovered by French archaeologists (ar-key-ol-o-jists). An Olympic enthusiast, Baron Pierre de Coubertin (coo-ber-tan) organized the first modern Olympics. The games were held in Greece in 1896.

Digging it
Archaeologists also uncovered the remains of the Olympians' training area, called the Palaestra (pal-eye-strah).

Fresh start
The first event of the 1896 Olympic Games was the 100-metre sprint, won by Thomas Burke (USA) in 12 seconds.

The greatest

"Faster!" shouted Coach Riley, looking down at his stopwatch as Jesse Owens hurtled past him. Jesse took giant strides, moving powerfully around the running track.

Coach Riley was Jesse's trainer in the early 1930s while he was at high school in Ohio, in the northeast of the United States.

Riley had never seen anyone with such natural athletic talent as Jesse, but his skills needed to be developed.

Riley taught Jesse special techniques to help him get the best sprint start, and to run with a smoother, quicker motion:

"Keep your head and body low and pump your arms hard, Jesse," said Riley.

"Now *bounce* off that track. Run like the ground is on fire!" he shouted to Jesse.

Good timing
Coach Riley's stopwatch could measure Jesse's speed to a tenth of a second. Modern stopwatches can measure a hundredth of a second.

Rising star
In this 1933 photograph, the young Jesse Owens wins the "220-yard dash" (200 metres) in an interschools competition.

It was 1933 and times were hard for most Americans. At home, Jesse's family struggled to make ends meet. Sometimes they didn't even have enough money for firewood. After school and at the weekends, Jesse delivered groceries in his neighbourhood to earn a little extra money for his family.

This meant that his hour-long training sessions had to take place early in the morning, before school started.

Jesse learnt fast and worked hard. His dedication paid off. In high school he entered 79 races and won an amazing 75 of them!

Team spirit
Jesse Owens with his American team-mates. In all, the US team took home 56 medals, 24 of which were gold!

In 1936, Jesse was thrilled to be chosen as part of the American team for the Berlin Olympic Games in Germany. Jesse was entered in three track events – the 100 metres, the 200 metres and the long jump.

The games took place in a huge new stadium. The Olympic torch was lit on Mount Olympus in Greece.

It was carried to Berlin by a series of runners. A crowd of 100,000 people cheered as the last runner carried the Olympic torch into the stadium.

Among the spectators was Adolf Hitler, the leader of Germany. He believed that athletes from his beloved home country would show the world their physical superiority. Could Jesse perform well enough to prove him wrong?

Six runners lined up for the final of the 100 metres.

"Around me are five of the fastest human beings on the planet and they all want to beat me to the finishing line," Jesse thought. "After all the training I've done since high school, everything rests on the next ten seconds."

Then he focused his mind on the track ahead.

11

"Bang!"

The starter fired his gun and the six finalists burst away from the "scratch" line. Jesse got a great start and began running smoothly. After just a few strides, he began to pull away from the pack, his faster running style eating up the ground in front of him.

Jesse blasted through the finishing line in 10.3 seconds – a time equal to the world record! Jesse had won his first gold medal.

The next day, Jesse returned to the stadium and ran into serious trouble while competing in the long jump. He had to do three jumps in his attempt to qualify for the final.

"Foul jump!" shouted the official, raising a red flag. For the second time Jesse's foot had gone over the edge of the takeoff board. If he fouled again, he'd be disqualified.

Jesse calmly retraced his steps back from the takeoff board, then turned and started the run up for his final jump. Jesse took off cleanly and sailed through the air.

Jump for joy
The best long jumpers are often superb sprinters. The faster the approach run, the longer the jump.

13

Friendly rivals
Luz Long befriended Jesse in full view of Hitler. Long gave Jesse valuable advice about how to avoid another foul jump.

Baton buddy
In a relay team there are four runners. Each runner sprints a 100-metre "leg" of the race, then passes on a baton to the next runner. The fastest runner in a team runs the last 100 metres.

Jesse landed in the sand pit at a distance good enough to qualify him for the long jump final. He breathed a quiet sigh of relief.

In the final, Jesse came head to head with his German rival, Luz Long. When Jesse set a new Olympic record with a jump of 8.06 metres (26 feet), it was Long who had to settle for the silver.

Two days later, Jesse won gold in the 200 metres with a time of 20.7 seconds, knocking a full half second off the previous best Olympic time. Jesse thought that his third gold medal would be his last, but a surprise was in store.

"We want you to run the last leg of the relay race," explained the manager of the American team. He thought that, with Jesse in the team, they couldn't lose.

He was right. The Americans triumphed, finishing 1.33 seconds ahead of the German team.

A sports writer described Jesse's run as being "as smooth as the west wind" – a fitting tribute to one of the greatest Olympians of all time.

Gold medal
Every Olympic competitor dreams of winning one gold medal. Swimmer Mark Spitz of the US won seven gold medals in 1972. No one yet has broken this record.

Berlin 1936
Very high standards were set at the 1936 Games. There were numerous world-record breakers. Owen's 8.06-metre long jump record remained unbeaten for 25 years!

15

In the swim of it

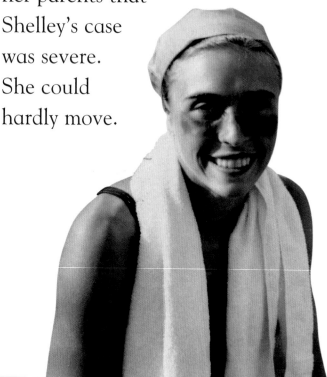

Some athletes have far greater challenges to face than beating their rivals on their way to success at the Olympics. To earn her Olympic medal, American Shelley Mann had to overcome a terrible disease that almost paralyzed her whole body.

The doctors looking after six-year-old Shelley in 1945 recognized the classic signs of polio. They told her parents that Shelley's case was severe. She could hardly move.

Healing waters
Many doctors recommend exercises in warm water to treat muscular illnesses.

Polio
Polio is a disease that affects part of the spinal cord and causes paralysis. All children should be vaccinated against polio.

At the age of ten, Shelley's family took her swimming at a summer camp in Maryland. She couldn't play golf or tennis with the other children, but she could mix with them in the pool.

Floating weightless in the warm water, Shelley began to move her weakened limbs.

"Lift your arms, Shelley. You can do it," her mother encouraged her.

Every day in the pool, Shelley worked to get the strength back in her body. It was difficult work, but swimming soon became the most important thing in her life.

At the age of twelve, Shelley began competitive training in Washington, DC. She was a natural at every stroke she tried.

Breaststroke

Front crawl

Backstroke

Butterfly

Racing strokes
At the time Shelley was training, breaststroke became the fourth stroke swum in competitions. In a medley race, swimmers did two lengths of each of the four strokes.

Dawn Fraser
Australia's Dawn Fraser swam in Sydney Harbour five hours a day to train for the Melbourne Olympics. She set the 100-metres freestyle record.

Butterfly
This is a symmetrical stroke, just like breaststroke. Swimmers use a strong, double-arm pull and a strong up and down "dolphin kick" with their legs.

One of the arm positions of the butterfly stroke

Shelley swam for an hour or more every day before and after school.

"I love to swim, and I love to win, so I work hard without knowing it," she said.

In the early 1950s, Shelley won the US National Championship for butterfly, backstroke, freestyle and medley races and was part of a record-breaking relay team. At the age of 17, Shelley found herself selected for the 1956 Olympic Games in Melbourne, Australia.

"You have to have the desire and you have to practise. Those are the two most important things," she said, just before the Games began.

She didn't begin well, coming sixth in the 100-metres freestyle.

In the 100-metres butterfly, Shelley stood waiting for the starter's signal. As the sound echoed around the pool, Shelley dived into the water, her powerful butterfly stroke propelling her down the pool. She touched home in a time of 1 minute 11 seconds, a new Olympic record.

As Shelley received her medal, tears ran down her face. Her hard work and willpower had paid off. The girl who couldn't move a muscle had struck gold.

Celebrity
After her Olympic win, Shelley Mann became a big celebrity. She travelled around the world, meeting thousands of people, but her heart was with her family. She said that her favourite place was "in a nice, warm bed with a cup of hot chocolate".

Shelley Mann, wearing the official uniform of the US Olympic team at the 1956 Olympics.

Never give up

Mamo Wolde pushed forward with his aching legs and forced himself to take another stride along the running track.

Mamo was on his last lap of the 10,000 metres at the 1964 Tokyo Games. More than anything else, he wanted to take home an Olympic medal for all his efforts.

He looked ahead and fixed his eyes on the runners in front of him. Using every last bit of strength, Mamo increased his speed and began gaining on them. However, as the three runners in front of him approached the finish line, they too increased their pace.

Mamo could only watch as the others won the medals. Though bitterly disappointed with fourth place, he walked over and congratulated the winner, American William Mills.

Get a grip!
Runners wear spiked shoes on Olympic stadium tracks. The spikes grip the rubber or plastic surface. Marathon runners don't wear spikes as they run on hard roads.

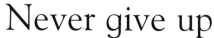

Spiked shoes

Marathon shoes

This was not Mamo's first Olympic defeat. In the 1956 Melbourne Games, Mamo had come last in the 10,000 metres. Now in the Tokyo stadium, Mamo watched Mills and the others receive their gold, silver and bronze medals on the rostrum.

"I am not finished yet," Mamo told himself. "I'll be back and going for gold in four years time."

TV winners
TV became popular in the late 1950s. Millions of people watched the 1964 Games on their sets.

Pasta

Potato

Peanuts

Athletes' diet
Top athletes, like Mamo eat a plain diet to maintain fitness. They eat starchy foods, like pasta and potatoes.

The high plains of Ethiopia, where Mamo trained with Abebe

Mamo returned home to Ethiopia in Africa and back to his job as a member of the Ethiopian Imperial Bodyguard.

Every day, Mamo went on a training run many miles across the rough, barren mountains.

Mamo's friend, Abebe Bikila, often joined him.

Abebe's Olympic career had been very different from Mamo's. Abebe had won the gold medal for the marathon at the last two Olympic Games. Abebe decided to give his good friend some advice.

One hot, dry evening the two men were jogging through the fading rays of an African sunset.

"Maybe the races you're running are too short for you?" suggested Abebe. "Your spirit wants to keep running. You should let it," he suggested.

"But I tried running a marathon once before and didn't even finish it," responded Mamo.

"So, try again until you do. One thing I've learned is never give up," said Abebe, before sprinting ahead. His simple words took root in Mamo's mind.

Abebe Bikila
Bikila was the first black athlete to win a marathon gold, at the 1960 Rome Games.

Abebe and Mamo training

High and dry
Mexico City is 2,300 metres (7,500 feet) above sea-level. Some athletes, like Mamo, were used to running on high terrain in the heat. Others suffered from altitude (height) sickness.

Marathon man
In 490 BC, a messenger ran 24 miles (38 kilometres) to report a Greek victory at the Battle of Marathon. This run inspired the first marathon.

Inspired by Abebe, Mamo made sure of his place in the starting line for the 1968 marathon in Mexico City.

Abebe Bikila was defending his title and was favourite to win. Mamo, however, had other ideas. He had planned his tactics.

As the race started, Mamo let some of the better-known athletes set the pace, but made sure that he was not far behind them.

About halfway through the 26-mile (41.6-kilometre) race, Mamo broke away from the rest and opened up a good lead. Abebe retired with a leg injury.

Mamo powered on. No matter how much his legs ached, no matter how hot and thirsty he became, uphill and down, he kept on running.

A modern marathon runner stops for a drink.

24

His willpower paid off and he entered the stadium to wild cheers. He was so far ahead that by the time the second runner had entered the stadium, Mamo had run round it in a "lap of honour" to celebrate his victory.

Mamo knew for sure that going for gold meant never giving up.

Mamo runs a lap of honour in the Mexico City stadium.

Four of the
ten decathlon
events are
track events:
100 metres,
400 metres,
1,500 metres,
110 metres
hurdles. The
other six are
field events:
the long
jump, high
jump, shot
put, discus,
javelin and
pole vault.

The rivals

Daley Thompson wiped the sweat
from his forehead. He stared up at
the giant scoreboard, waiting for his
winning time in the 100-metre
sprint, the first event in the 1984
Los Angeles Olympics decathlon.

Decathletes are ultimate
sportsmen and women. They
compete in a gruelling two-day
series of ten track and field events.
They score points for their
performance in each event – the
athlete with the most points wins.

*Ball used
for the
shot put*

*Only one hand
may be used to
throw the shot.
This hand must
be in front of
the shoulders.*

*The athlete
throws the
javelin as far
as he can.*

Thompson had won the decathlon gold medal in Moscow in 1980. He was determined to write himself into history as the second man to win two decathlon golds.

Thompson's 100-metre time of 10.44 seconds flashed up on the board. He waved to the crowd, knowing how much his fans enjoyed watching him. He also knew that, to win the competition, he'd have to give the performance of a lifetime. He had an arch-rival and it was showdown time.

Moscow 1980
Every Olympic Games now has a mascot. The first was a red jaguar for the Mexican Games in 1968. The mascot for Moscow in 1980 was Misha the Bear.

The athlete spins around to throw the discus.

An athlete must leap 10 hurdles in any hurdle race. He is not disqualified for knocking down a hurdle.

LA style
The opening ceremony of the 1984 Games was amazing, with marching bands and a display of flags from nations taking part.

Rivals
British runners, Steve Ovett and Sebastian Coe competed fiercely in 1980 and 1984. Coe eventually won more medals.

Jurgen Hingsen was a huge, powerfully built West German decathlete. He had stolen the decathlon world record from Thompson twice before.

Before Thompson had arrived at the Los Angeles Games, newspaper reporters had asked him if he felt threatened by Hingsen.

"There's only one way Hingsen's going to take a gold medal home. He'll have to steal mine," Thompson replied.

Hingsen had come third in the 100 metres and Thompson had also beaten him in the long jump. But the battle had only just begun – Hingsen fought back. He did better in the shot put than Thompson and won the high jump competition with a jump of 2.12 metres (7 ft).

The punishing duel continued on the morning of the second day, when the crowd watched a thrilling 110-metre hurdle race. The two athletes hurtled neck and neck down the track. Thompson's fans rose to their feet to see Hingsen beat him by just 0.04 seconds.

Hingsen also beat Thompson by a whisker in the hurdle race of the 1983 Helsinki World Athletics Championships in Finland.

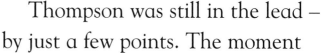

Thompson was still in the lead – by just a few points. The moment that decided the great battle finally came in the discus competition. Thompson fouled his first two throws, while Hingsen achieved a huge distance of 50.82 metres (167 ft).

Ancient Greek discus

Discus
The discus dates back to the eighth century BC. The modern discus is made of wood with a metal rim.

Discus throw
The athlete releases the discus after turning.
The throw has to take place from inside a cage to avoid accidents.

If Thompson fouled his last throw, his rival would take the lead. Thompson thrived under the pressure. He knew that his fans were on the edges of their seats, wondering what he would do next. He picked up the discus and lined himself up in the throwing circle, concentrating hard. Then, with all his strength, he spun around and propelled the discus far into the air. It was a clean throw. He had scored a distance of 46.56 metres (152.7 ft), not enough to beat Hingsen, but enough to keep his overall lead.

After that, Thompson could do no wrong. He beat Hingsen in the pole vault and the javelin, although Hingsen did better in the 1,500 metres, ensuring he won the silver medal. Thompson hadn't beaten Hingsen's world record but he didn't care – he'd won the gold! "People don't remember world records," he said. "They remember Olympic champions."

Pole vault
In this event, the athlete pushes off from the ground, bends the pole with his weight, and levers himself over the bar.

Superstar
Jurgen Hingsen said of his rival: "Daley is truly the greatest among us, for he has no weaknesses."

31

Game, set and match

American Jennifer Capriati began playing tennis at the age of three when her father gave her a racquet. He soon realized just how talented she was and dedicated his time to coaching her.

Jennifer was a tennis star by the age of 15. She beat Martina Navratilova in 1991 to become the youngest-ever female semi-finalist at Wimbledon. A year later, she stood on a clay court in the Spanish sunshine and looked up at the faces in the crowd.

"I'm the underdog. They're expecting me to lose," she thought. The teenager was about to play the most important match of her life – the tennis final of the 1992 Barcelona Olympic Games in Spain.

Jennifer stepped on to the court. Waiting for her on the other side was the formidable figure of Steffi Graf.

Spanish village
The city hosting the Olympics builds a "village" with hotels for athletes and a stadium for the competition.

Racquets
New, hi-tech racquets send balls much faster than the old, wooden racquets could.

German-born Steffi was the world's number two female player. Jennifer had played Steffi four times before and had lost every time.

Steffi had not lost a set on the way to this Olympic final. The two women stood on either side of the net like ancient gladiators.

Steffi started well, hitting powerful volleys into the outer corners of the court. Jennifer stretched to return them when she could, but Steffi won the first set 6–3.

Winner
Steffi Graf had just won the world-famous British tennis competition, Wimbledon, for a fourth time.

Feet of clay
Outdoor tennis matches are played on grass or on clay. The Olympic court was a clay court. Jennifer played better on clay which has a faster surface.

Best shot
Steffi was amazed by Jennifer's powerful and accurate double-handed backhands.

Smashing
A smash is the most powerful tennis stroke. A player needs confidence and concentration to hit a good smash. Steffi probably has the best smash of any female player.

Instead of giving up hope, Jennifer started the second set with increased determination and energy. If Steffi played a forehand smash, Jennifer raced to the back of the court to return it. If Steffi fired off a forehand drive, Jennifer used her double-handed backhand to get the ball back low over the net. Jennifer won the second set 6–3.

The third and final set was finely balanced and Steffi's play forced her young opponent to find new reserves of willpower and mental as well as physical strength.

The player leans back before she hits.

She jumps up to the ball in front of her.

She brings the racquet down hard on the ball.

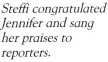

Jennifer's challenge to Steffi Graf had captivated the crowd. Every point that Jennifer won was greeted by wild cheers.

Jennifer won the next three games in a row and the umpire finally called, "Game, set and match to Miss Capriati!"

Jennifer's gold medal victory was one of the biggest Olympic upsets for years. Steffi had met her match in a tough teenager. Jennifer had clung on to her dream of gold to become the youngest-ever Olympic tennis gold medallist.

Spanish star
Jennifer had started playing tennis on a family holiday in Spain. Barcelona was therefore a fitting place for her to become a champion.

Steffi congratulated Jennifer and sang her praises to reporters.

Atlanta mascot
Atlanta's organizers had to contend with two million visitors and had to look after 15,500 athletes.

Press gangs
Press and TV reporters from all the competing countries gathered for the opening ceremony.

Pain and glory

"Do you really think you can do it? Can America win gold?" asked the TV reporter from *Atlanta News*, thrusting a microphone at Kerri Strug. The cameras flashed.

"This is the best women's gymnastics team we've ever had," said Kerri to the crowd of over a hundred reporters gathered around her. "We're good enough to do it," she grinned.

Leaving the press behind, Kerri quickly rejoined her team-mates as they set off by bus for their final training session. There were only a few days until the 1996 Olympics in Atlanta, Georgia, USA. Pressure was mounting on the girls to do well. The national newspapers already had a great headline.

Kerri and her six team-mates were named "The Magnificent Seven".

The last year had been hard work for the girls. Kerri, like the others, had been locked away with her coach, Bela Karolyi, practising exercise after exercise. She had performed her routines on the bars, beam, floor and vault until she knew them backwards.

"In a few days," Kerri said to herself, "it will be time to show the world what we can do."

Hard work
At his gym in Houston, Texas, Kerri's coach Bela Karolyi made her train for eight hours a day, six days a week.

Spectacle
President Clinton opened the 1996 Games in Atlanta. The opening ceremony was spectacular.

In team gymnastics, each team member is given a score out of 10. The best scores are added up and averaged.

The gymnast swings and circles on the bars.

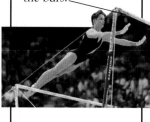

The gymnast walks, leaps and balances on the beam.

In a vault, the gymnast runs up to the horse. Then she pushes off from it doing twists and somersaults.

The "vaulting horse" is covered with smooth leather.

There was a huge roar of support from the home crowd when Kerri and the team walked out into the Georgia Dome for the first day's competition. The gymnastics began with the bars, before moving on to the beam event.

"We're third behind Russia and Romania," reported Bela, as Kerri stepped out to perform her floor routine. Kerri's floor moves lit up the stadium and she scored 9.825 – enough to help move America up into second place.

The Americans had never beaten the Russians to an Olympic team gold medal in gymnastics. That night, Kerri wrote in her diary, "The team's all ready. Tomorrow we're going for the gold!"

On the next and final day, after more bar and floor exercises, America was in the lead.

The team was thrilled. Only the vault – Kerri's best event – now stood between them and a gold medal.

In her floor routine, Kerri delighted the audience and the judges with her dynamic "tumbling runs" and her sense of fun.

Dominique
Dominique Moceanu was a stunning performer. She was the all-round national champion in 1995.

Perfection
In 1976, Romanian Nadia Comaneci became the first gymnast ever to score a "Perfect 10". On seven occasions each judge gave her ten points.

The first two American girls only achieved average marks on the vault. At the same time, the Russians were producing their best performances so far on the floor.

Kerri watched as team-mate Dominique Moceanu (mo-cho-noo) ran up for her first vault. Dominique twisted through the air gracefully. As she landed, however, she suddenly fell.

"Forget it, forget it!" ordered Bela, the coach, but everyone could see the shocked look on Dominique's face. She ran in again for her second vault. Kerri could hardly bear to watch as Dominique fell again. This was a disaster.

A breathless hush fell over the Dome as the crowd realized that the Russians, who were still enchanting the audience with their floor routines, were catching up.

These pictures show a basic vaulting sequence.

The gymnast manages a good, high takeoff.

She pushes off the horse…

…and lands cleanly.

Yurchenko
To perform a Yurchenko, the gymnast somersaults onto the horse, somersaults again, then pushes off and twists in the air.

It was now all up to Kerri. She walked to her starting position.

She was going to perform the difficult "Yurchenko" vault.

"You know you can do it," Kerri told herself as she began her run in. Her team-mates were depending on her.

Kerri somersaulted onto the horse, pushed off and twisted beautifully in mid-air. She began to open her arms for the landing position. But Kerri had misjudged the distance to the floor mat.

Big risk
Gymnasts are most likely to get injured on the vault or the bars because these exercises strain their wrist and ankle joints.

She hit the ground sooner than she expected and toppled backwards. Another fall! One fall in the vault event was almost unheard of for a team – but three in a row?

As Kerri picked herself up from the floor mat, a sharp pain shot through her left foot.

"You can do it. One more. You can do it, Kerri," she heard Bela saying. She fought back the tears.

As Kerri limped back to the run-up area, she knew her ankle was badly injured. She knew she should withdraw from the competition. But she also knew that her team needed her second vault. It had to be good.

Kerri ran in again, terrified of falling in front of the billion people watching in the stadium and on TV. This time she twisted through the air and landed cleanly. She went into the finishing position, but a second later she collapsed in agony. Despite terrible pain Kerri had scored 9.712 – enough for the American team to stay in the lead.

End of an era
The 1996 Olympics in Atlanta were the last Games of the 20th century. They ended with a huge fireworks display.

"You did it!" beamed Bela. He carried her in his arms to the medal ceremony. Bela held Kerri as she collected her gold medal and the crowd cheered on and on.

Sydney 2000

Sydney 2000

The year 2000 Olympics will be the most spectacular ever. They will be held in Sydney, Australia, and involve more than 10,000 athletes from 200 countries around the globe, as well as 5,000,000 spectators.

New Olympic sports will include taekwondo (tie-kwon-doe) and the triathlon.

More than 3.5 billion people are expected to watch the Games on TV.

Opening ceremony:
Friday, September 15, 2000

Closing ceremony:
Sunday, October 1, 2000

Different sports

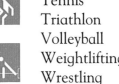

Aquatics
Archery
Athletics
Badminton
Baseball
Basketball
Boxing
Canoe/kayak
Cycling
Equestrian
Fencing
Football
Gymnastics
Handball
Hockey
Judo
Pentathlon
Rowing
Sailing
Shooting
Softball
Table tennis
Taekwondo
Tennis
Triathlon
Volleyball
Weightlifting
Wrestling

Sydney celebrates

When Australia won its bid to host the Olympic Games in 2000 the Australians were overjoyed. They celebrated with dazzling firework displays over Sydney Harbour.

Officials:

Total number of Olympic officials: 5,100

Village

This will have 477 houses and more than 330 units to house 15,300 people.

Money

Cost of hosting the Games: A$2.6 billion

Olympic record breakers

Most medals

Most gold medals
10 Raymond Ewry (you-ree) (USA)
Standing, high, long and triple
jumps, 1900, 1904, 1906, 1908

Most medals in total (female)
18 Larisa Latynina (la-tee-nee-na)
(USSR – gymnastics) 1956–64

Most medals in total (male)
15 Nikolay (nik-oh-lie) Adrianov
(USSR – gymnastics) 1972–1980

Most gold medals won in one Games
7 Mark Spitz (USA – swimming,
including three medals for relays) 1972

Most medals by nation

1	United States	2,015
2	Soviet Union	1,234
3	Great Britain	635
4	France	562
5	Germany*	516
6	Sweden	459
7	Italy	444
8	Hungary	425
9	East Germany*	410
10	Australia	294

*Germany split into West
Germany and East Germany
between 1968 and 1988.

Track Olympic and world records

100 metres: 9.84 seconds – Donovan Bailey (Canada), Atlanta 1996

200 metres: 19.32 seconds – Michael Johnson (USA), Atlanta 1996

400 metres: 43.86 seconds – Lee Evans (USA), Mexico City 1968

1,500 metres: 3 minutes 35.6 seconds – Herb Elliot (Australia),
Rome 1960

10,000 metres: 27 minutes 38.4 seconds – Lasse Viren (Finland),
Montreal 1976

The fastest woman ever was Florence Griffith-Joyner (USA)
who ran at 39.56 kilometres per hour (24.58 miles per hour)
in the women's 100-metres final in Seoul, South Korea, 1988.

Youngest and oldest

Youngest competitor
7-10 years old:
unknown French boy
used by the Dutch rowing
team in 1900

Youngest gold medallist
13 years old:
Marjorie Gestring
(USA – diving) 1936

Oldest competitor
72 years old: Oscar Swahn
(Sweden – shooting) 1920

Oldest female competitor
70 years old: Lorna
Johnstone (Great Britain –
equestrian) 1972

Oldest gold medallist
60 years old: Oscar Swahn
(Sweden – shooting) 1908

Fun Olympic facts

• Mongolia is the nation whose athletes have won most medals (13) but never a gold!

• Roswitha Krause (krow-se) (GDR) is the only woman to have won medals in two sports: 1968 – swimming 1976–80 – athletics

• Daniel Carroll won rugby gold medals for two countries: 1908 Australia, 1920 USA

• In 1992, Russian gymnast Vitaly Scherbo (sher-bow) won four gold medals in a single day.

• In 1988, Byun Jong II (bee-yun yong second) of South Korea staged the longest protest about a judge's decision. He remained in the boxing ring for one hour and seven minutes, even after the lights had been switched off.

• Only three countries have competed in every Olympic Games – Australia, France and Greece.

• The most competitors at a summer games is 10,744 (7,060 men, 3,684 women) at Atlanta, USA, 1996.

Glossary

Archaeologist
Someone who studies ancient times and peoples by examining what is left of their buildings, tools, weapons and art.

Ceremony
A series of acts done in a special way to celebrate an occasion.

Chariot
A horse-drawn cart raced on a racetrack in ancient Rome.

Coach
A person who teaches and trains athletes and performers.

Discipline
In sport, a particular event for which an athlete trains.

Disqualify
To stop an athlete taking part in an event because they have broken a rule.

Foul
An act that breaks the rules of a game or athletic event.

Freestyle
In a swimming race, "freestyle" means that the competitor can use any stroke. This is most often front crawl, the fastest stroke.

Gladiator
A man of ancient Rome who used to fight men or animals to entertain the crowds.

Host
A person or people who provide guests with places of comfort and entertainment in their home or city.

Mascot
A person, animal or thing that is supposed to bring someone good luck.

Motto
A brief saying that is used as a rule to live by, including a rule that encourages true sportsmanship.

Olympian
A man or woman who competes in the Olympic Games.

Paralysis
A medical condition in which the person loses feeling in a part, or all, of their body.

Qualify
To get good enough results to go forward to the final stages of a competition.

Rival
A person who tries to do better than another.

Routine
A series of steps for a dance or gymnastic performance; a regular way of doing something, fixed by rules or habit.

Spectator
A person who watches something without taking part.

Sprint
To run at full speed.

Stadium
A building that is used for outdoor athletic events and displays.

Tactic
A skilful method used by a person or team to help them succeed in a task or a sport.

Umpire
A person who ensures that a game is played fairly and according to the rules.

Underdog
A person, team or side that is expected to lose a contest of some kind.

Willpower
A strength of will, mind or purpose.